Make & color your own
Christmas
Decorations

By Jill E. Osborne

Watermill Press

Make & color your own

Christmas Decorations

Here's what you need:

scissors

crayons

felt markers

colored pencils

string, thread, or yarn

sequins

cotton

glue

Here's what you do:

1. Tear out a page from the book. Be careful—don't rip it!

2. Color the Christmas shapes. Don't forget to do both sides!

3. Glue on cotton or sequins if you want to make your decoration extra-special.

4. Cut out shapes.

5. Punch hole in top of each shape.

6. Pull string, thread, or yarn through the hole.

7. Tie onto your Christmas tree!

Make sure all paper Christmas ornaments are away from hot tree bulbs.

Suggested uses:

hang decorations

paste on greeting cards

mobiles

gift tags

place mats

place cards

mailbox

paste on tablecloths

angels

candy canes
& stars

Christmas balls

Make your own design.

Christmas trees

Decorate this tree yourself!

gingerbread
people

reindeer

Santa
Claus

snowflakes

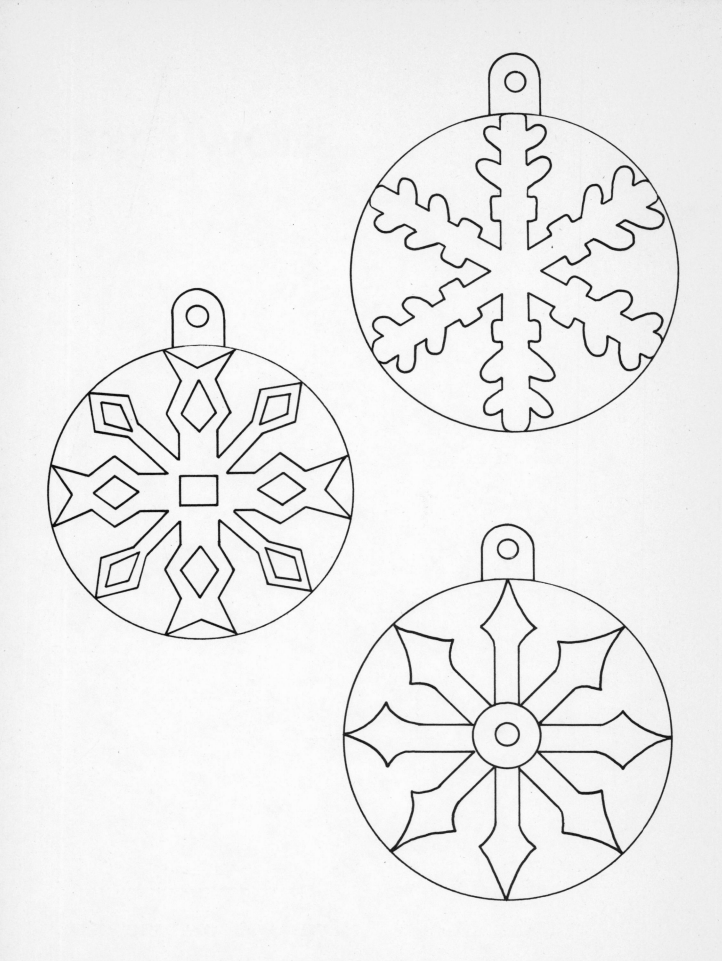

snowmen

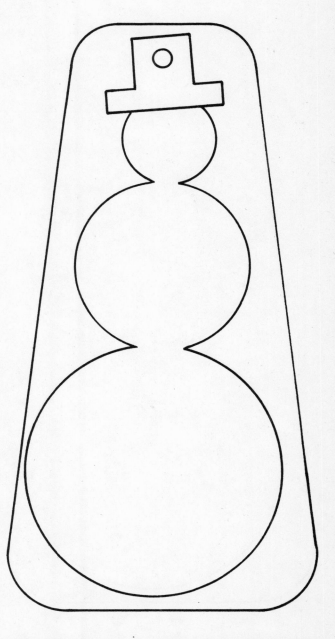

Draw your own snowman!

stars &
snowflakes

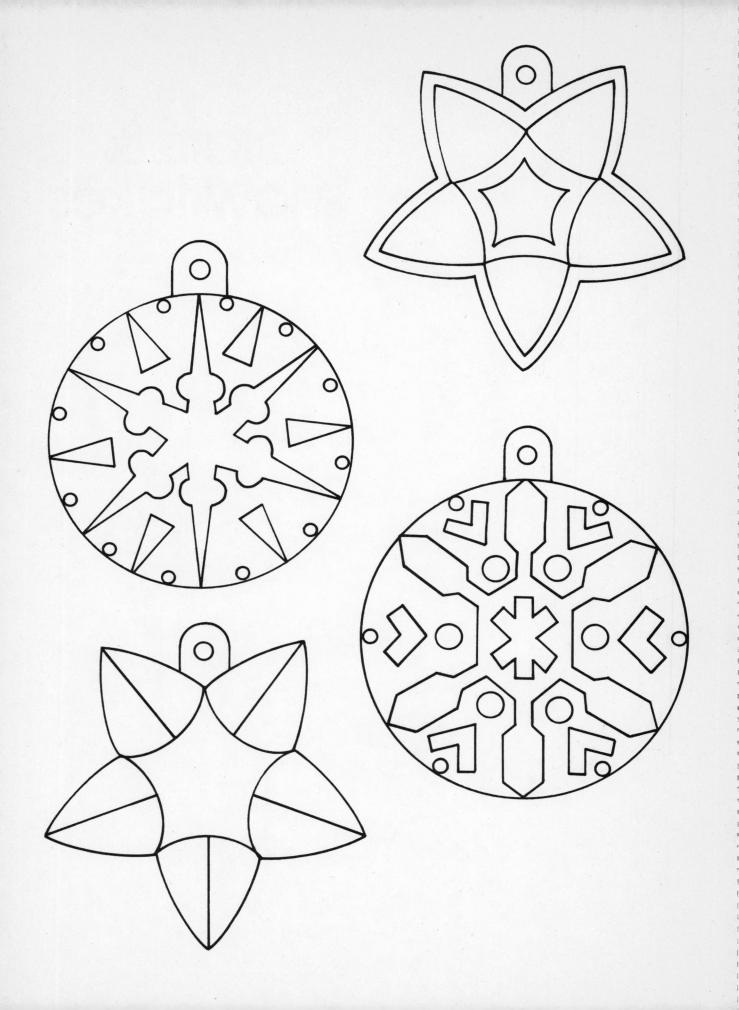

stocking

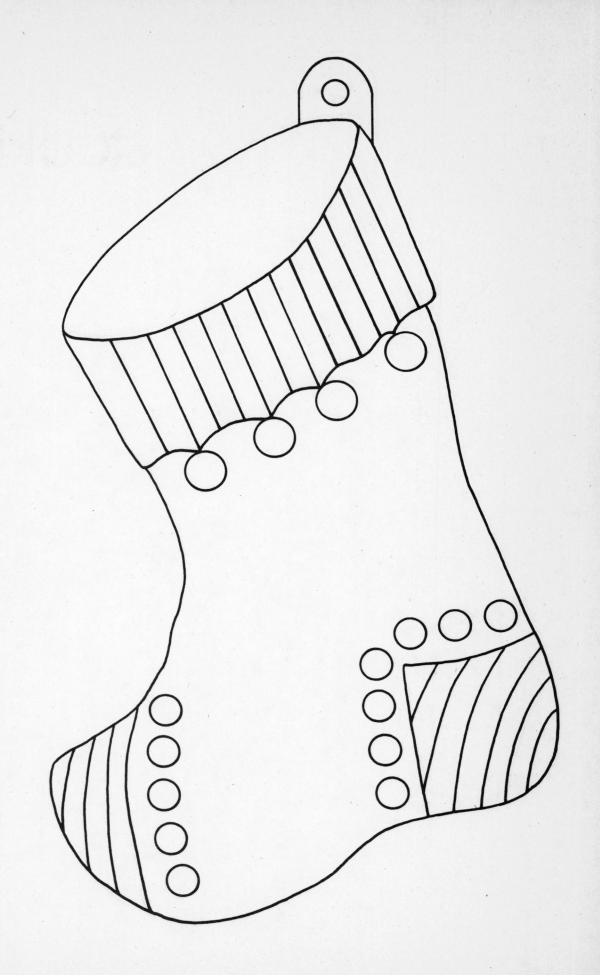

toy soldiers

trains &
horses

bells

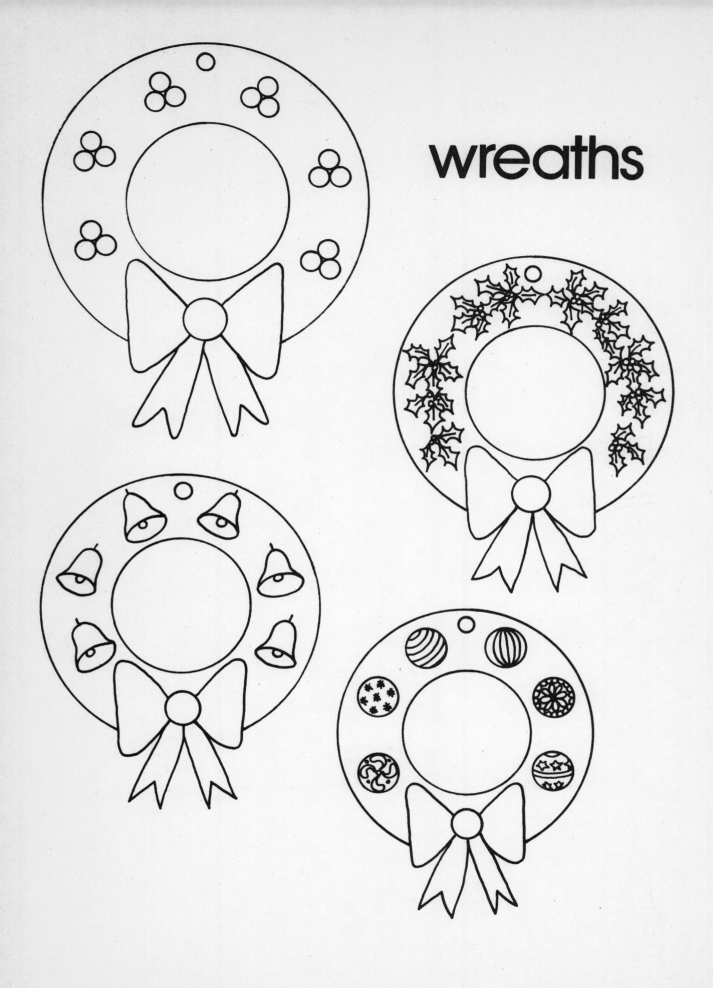

wreaths